This book belongs to:

TINY
TREEHOUSE
PUBLISHING

HAPPY HALLOWEEN

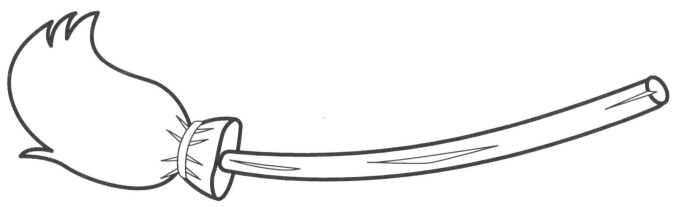

TRICK OR TREAT

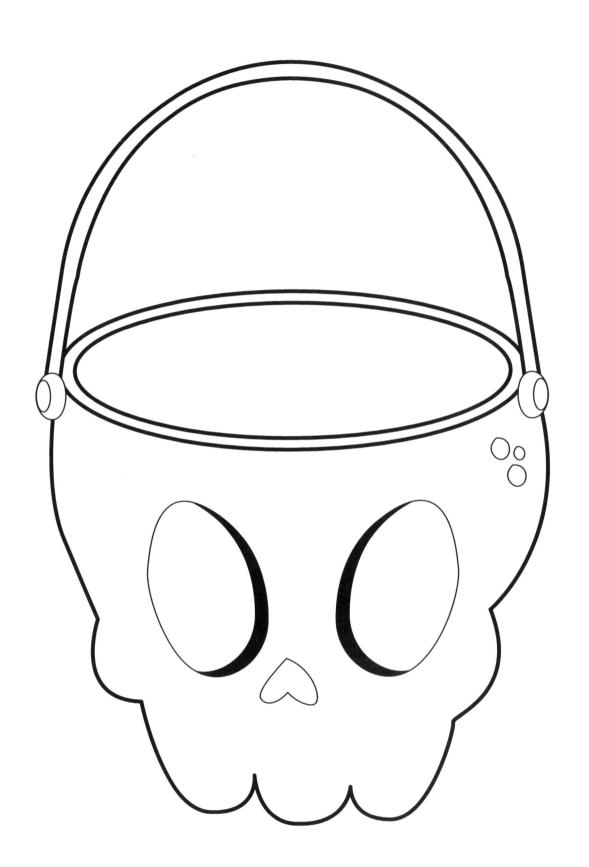

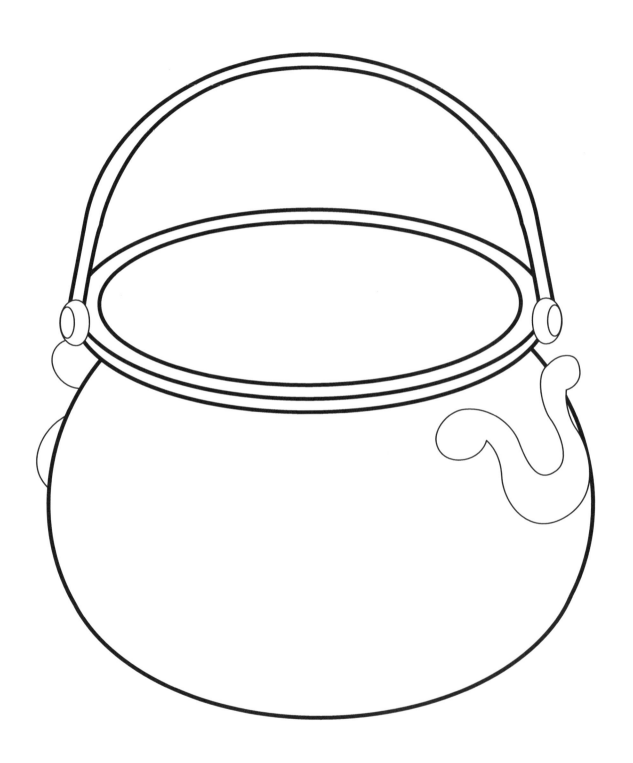

DOG

CAT

BAT

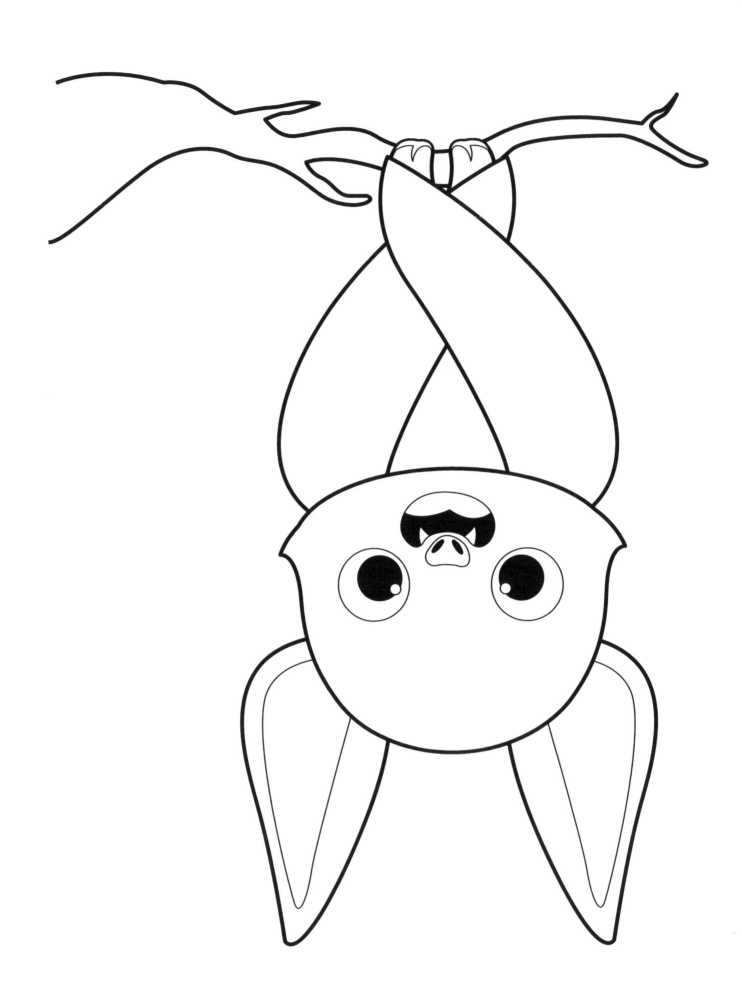

HAT

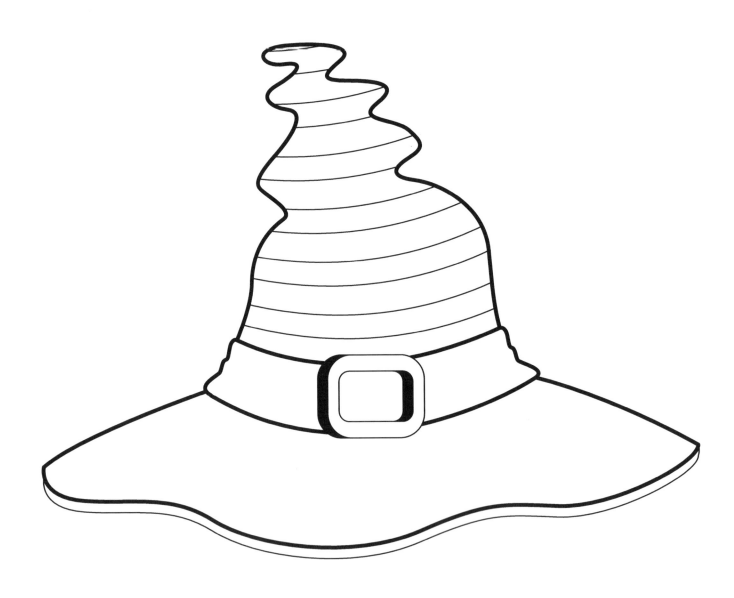

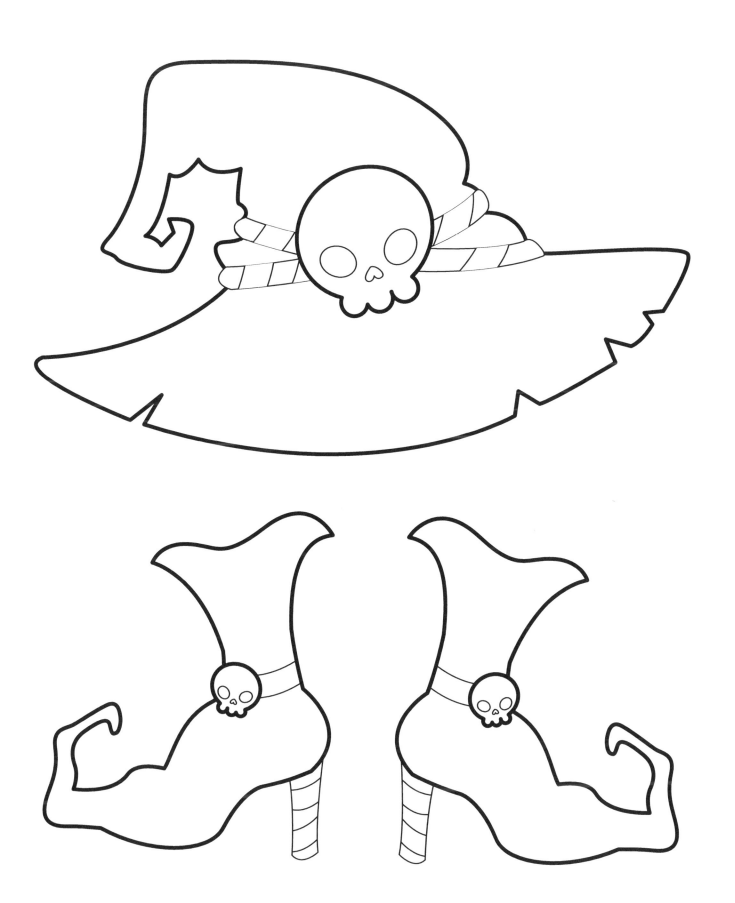

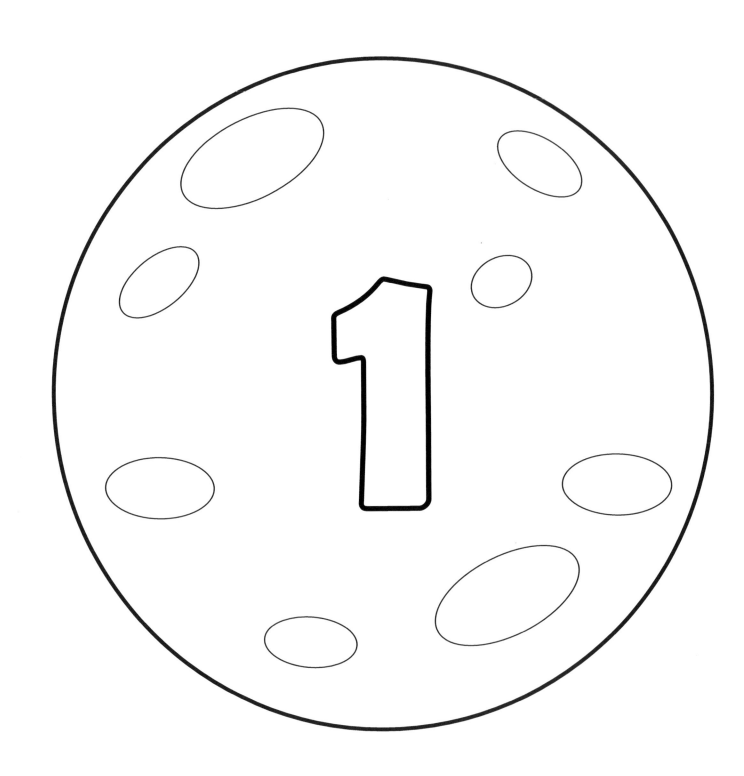

2

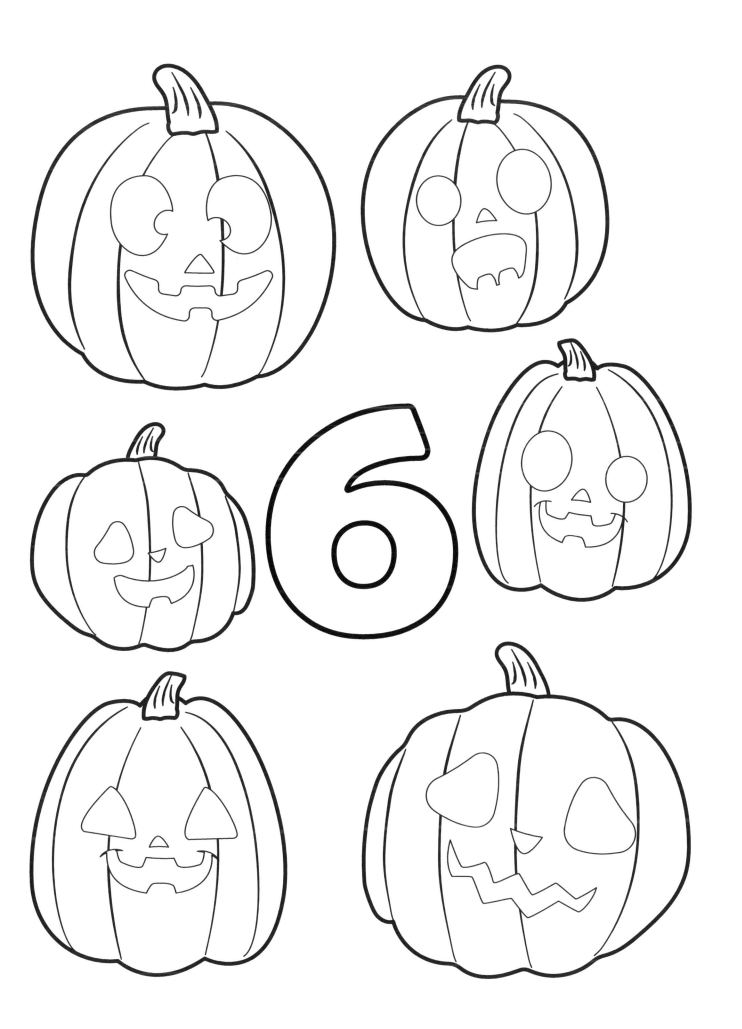

EEK

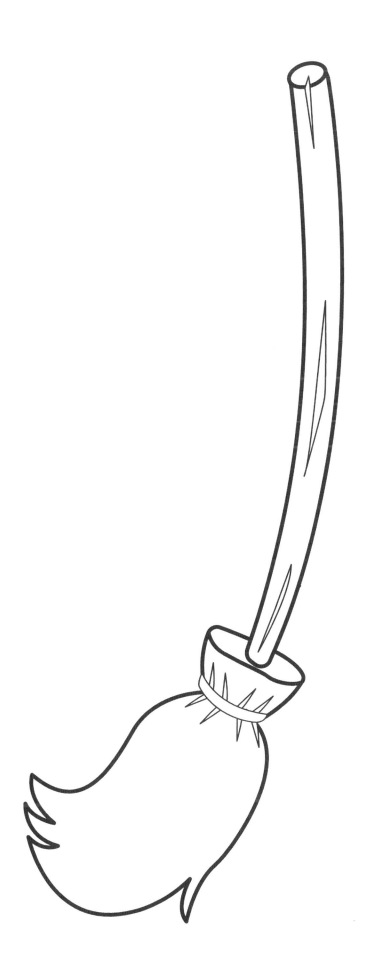

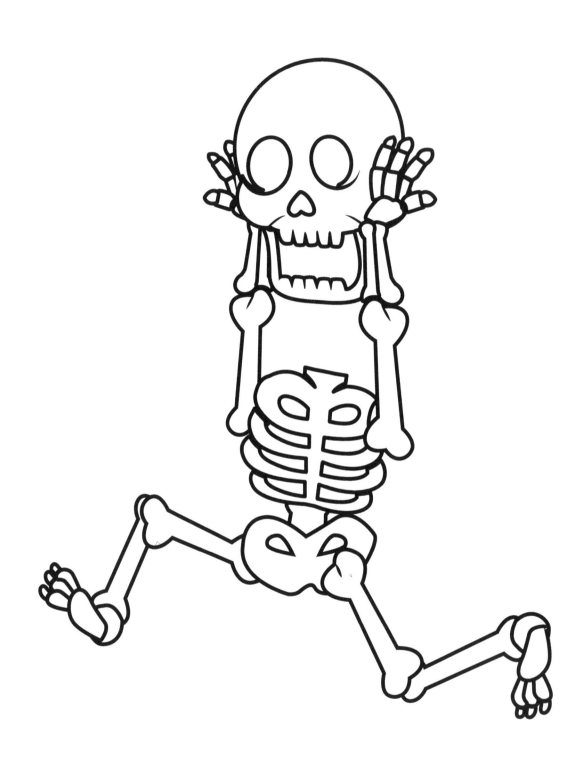

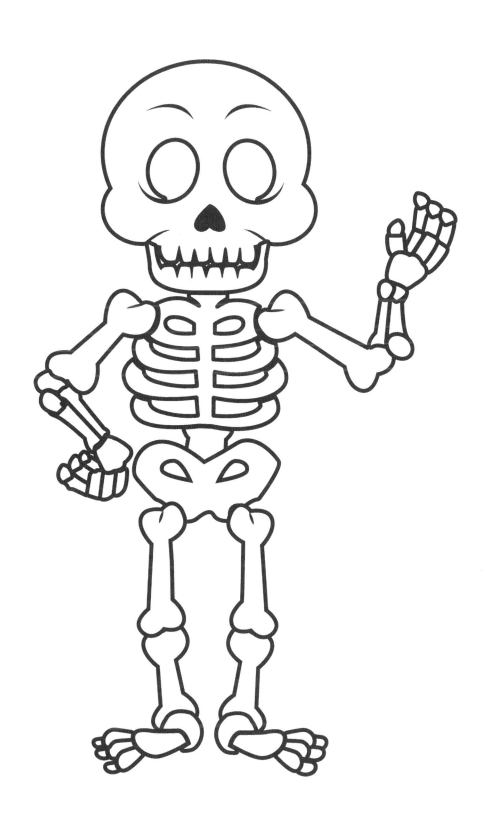

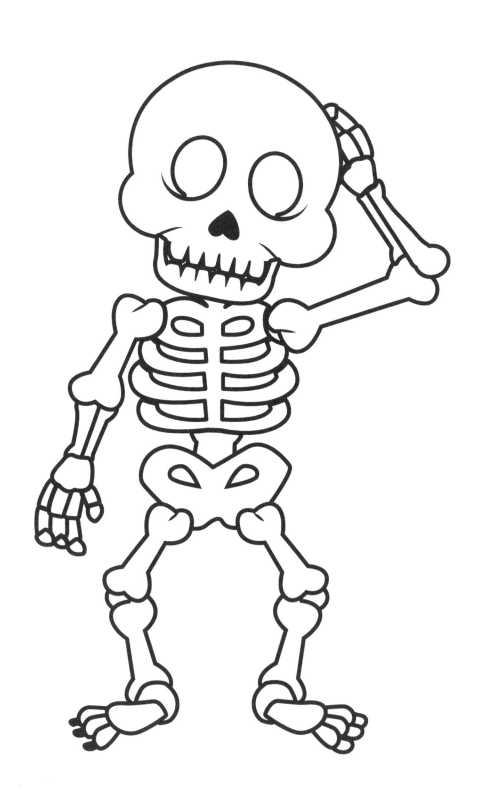

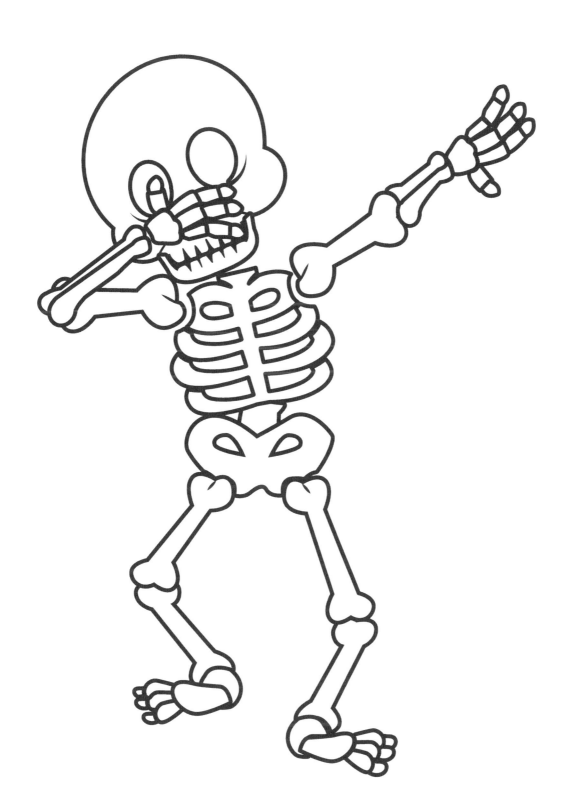

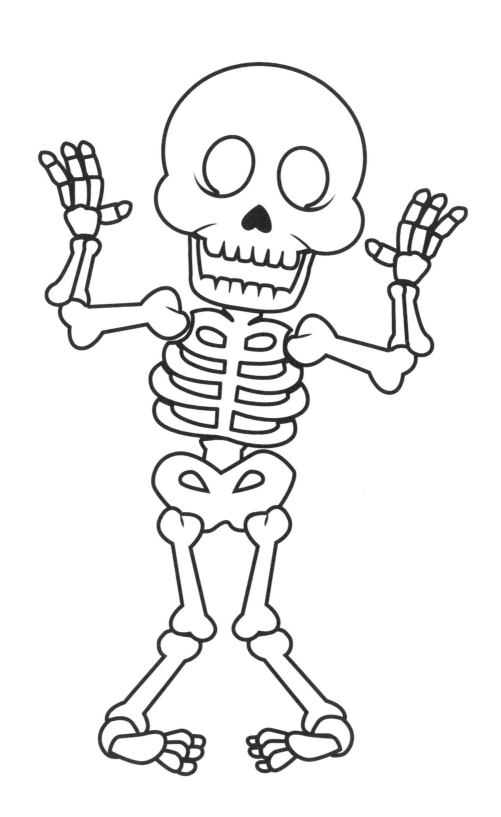

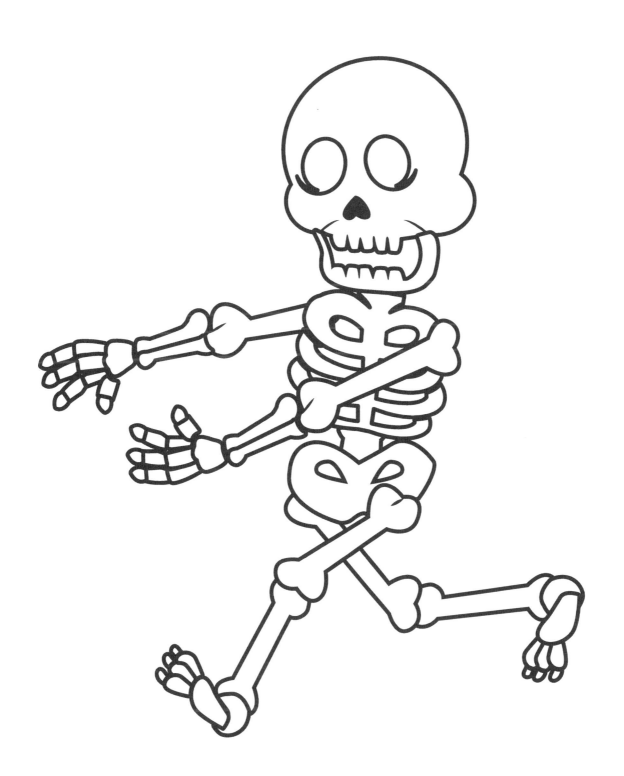

OWL

Did your family enjoy this book?

Please consider leaving a review. This is the first coloring book I have created, and I would love to hear your feedback!

Thank you!

Want the fun to continue?

Email TinyTreehousePublishing@gmail.com with the subject "Halloween Freebee" to receive more halloween coloring sheets for your little one to enjoy.

Made in the USA
Monee, IL
20 October 2023

44896063R00059